"Astonishing! I have never beheld ¿ the wild earth, to its unbounded elegance and heart-wrenching vulnerability, to its singular ability to penetrate our carefully shielded minds and deliver us directly into the arms of a love that lives in every cell of our bodies. These poems – these prayers – make me want to throw off my shoes, take down my hair and run into the woods. Then walk very slowly, lie down for a while, pay attention like I have never before paid attention. I thirst for the elixir Sharifa offers. I want everyone I know to drink deeply and be transfigured by the sacred wonderment shining from every nexus of these beautifully written poems." —**Mirabai Starr, Translator of the great mystics and author of** *Caravan of No Despair: A Memoir of Loss & Transformation* **and** *Wild Mercy: Living the Fierce & Tender Wisdom of the Women Mystics*

"Sharifa Oppenheimer's Gaian hymns bear exquisite witness to the sacred mystery that flashes, murmurs, flutters, and blooms beyond the bounds of human 'progress.' In these pages, we are evocatively reminded of a world that has always been ravishingly whole and unutterably lovely." —**Pir Zia Inayat Khan, author of** *Saracen Chivalry*, *Mingled Waters*, **and** *Immortality*

"In the poetry of Sharifa Oppenheimer you will hear the living voices of the natural world calling out to us. So many people today live in the midst of the deafening, hollow, numbing racket of our contemporary soulless world. Sharifa awakens us again to the natural abundance of life's music, which arises from the Earth at every moment. Her message so beautifully expresses what is the essential practice for us at this time, and I find refuge, relief and reassurance in it. So many life forms have already been lost and many more are in present danger. Sharifa can teach us how to hear and respond to their songs and pleas; how to embrace the wholeness of our human journey. Thank you Sharifa, for honoring your call to write, so we may realize again that we are part of a living planet. Share these poems with as many people as possible." —**Atum Okane, is the founder and director of the international Spiritual Guidance Wisdom School**

"*A Litany of Wild Graces* is a call to experience a sensuous encounter with the living Universe. Poems, essays and litanies are imbued with hymns to botany, biology, geography, cosmology and all life, inviting us to engage deeply, to create pathways of loving and honoring our sacred earth. When I received this manuscript, I went outside and opened it as a ritual under my favorite tree. Suddenly a large flock of birds made three wide circles over my head; a beautiful ayat ~ a sign ~ from the birds! Receive the grace and blessing of this beautiful book." —Felicia Kainat Norton ~ author of *An Emerald Earth*, Senior teacher, Director Emeritus of Ziraat, Inayatiyya Order

"*A Litany of Wild Graces* takes us into the unseen territories of nature. In both her prose and poetry, Sharifa Oppenheimer walks us through interiors of mountains, under the bark of trees and alongside sun and stardust and minerals. This collection of Sharifa's work brings comfort and companionship to all of us who steward the earth." —Barbara Shinn, biodynamic farmer and vintner, owner of Shinn Estate Vineyards

"Whether to honor and revel in the myriad beauties of the world, or to mend our grieving souls, we will find this and more in Sharifa Oppenheimer's words of praise for all that is. The unseen and inexplicable have found their reverent muse. *A Litany of Wild Graces* intertwines the sacred and quotidian with the urgency of now, to not only celebrate but also call us to reimagine our relationship to the Earth of which we are an integral part. Sharifa's Litany, her profound project, gives me hope." —Paige Hartsell, Education and Outreach Coordinator, Pfeiffer Biodynamics

"Sharifa's devotional poems and essays define the need to be conscious of the reality of all-world-connectedness. Never in human history has this understanding been more needed. As we face our unjust and troubled world where, as she states 'the past is imprisoned behind us and the future walks before wielding whips.' Clearly we must wake up as defenders of our Mother Earth as She withers and rebels before our global desecration.

No one speaks with more grace, beauty and authenticity. May we unite together as in Sharifa's prayerful plea for 'the human community to be woven together for a sacred moment outside of time.' Together we can be the transcendent forces for the good, the beautiful, and the true that our times call for!"—Nancy Jewel Poer, co-founder of Rudolf Steiner College, author of *Living Into Dying*

A Litany
of
Wild Graces

MEDITATIONS ON SACRED ECOLOGY

SHARIFA OPPENHEIMER

Red Elixir
Rhinebeck, New York

Paperback ISBN 978-1-954744-62-2
eBook ISBN 978-1-954744-63-9

Library of Congress Control Number 2022903978

Book design by Colin Rolfe
Front cover painting: "Rays of Sunlight Striking a Woodland Path"
(c. 1815) by Friedrich Salathé

Red Elixir is an imprint of Monkfish Book Publishing Company

Red Elixir
22 East Market Street, Suite 304
Rhinebeck, NY 12572
monkfishpublishing.com

Acknowledgments

May I give thanks with each breath to the great grace and mystery that has placed my life and the lives of all beings into this shimmering sphere, this verdant mother from whom all life emerges and to whom we all return.

I would like to acknowledge the Monacan Nation, the original and present keepers of the land and waters in Virginia, the place I call home. I give gratitude as well to First Nations people worldwide. They not only continue to hold crucial knowledge, both spiritual and scientific, but they also are at the forefront, shielding Earth and her other-than-human members from the onslaught of human destruction.

Much gratitude to the countless living beings who inhabit this mountain forest side by side with my human family. They teach us goodness, beauty, reciprocity, generosity, joy, persistence, forbearance, resilience, truth and so much more. They are the *living* litany of wild graces.

Endless thanks to my beloved friend Asha Greer, who was the first to hear every poem, who joined me in years of conversation and forest walks. She lives now in the spirit world, where she tends the wild with a subtle hand.

To Robin Luecke who has a seamlessly fine-drawn editorial pen, and Ralph Earle, whose questions and nudges were reliable navigational tools.

To my lovely husband Eric, who has walked beside me, helped in innumerable ways and from the very beginning, even when I faltered, has always believed I could.

Many thanks to Red Elixir Press, especially Paul Cohen and Colin Rolfe, for bringing this book into the world.

To the Reader

These verses are prayers ~ words of honor and thanksgiving ~ to the myriad beings seen and unseen, with whom I share life in this still-healthy Virginia woodland. I write for my other-than-human friends who speak in languages I, only now, am learning to understand. Sometimes I walk the forest paths and speak or sing these prayers to the trees in the oxygen-rich air they have made for me, knowing human language will not translate. But the meaning and my heart will.

It has not been often that I share these words with human friends, but one summer day I took the sheaf of verse to someone who might understand. Windows down, I drove through the hills lit by a hundred shades of green. A bee suddenly came in; I reached for the folder of papers to usher her back out. A rush of wind, and out into the emerald-soaked sunlight, strewn across the fern and moss-carpeted forest floor, caught by prickly wine berry canes, and hung between looping grapevines draped among poplar branches, white sheets of paper began their return home to their primeval forested state. I had spoken and sung them to the forest, before, but now they were truly *given*. Perhaps we are all prayers being spoken into life; when we are *fully given*, we also return to our original state.

They are enchantments. These words are written for you the reader, as well. They have dressed themselves in silk spun by mulberry worms, have rouged their lips and cheeks. They wear a subtle musky perfume and beckon. Come close ~ lie down in the generous arms of the wild. She is exhilarating, nurturing, dangerous, essential. *She is life.* She is calling you:

> Come to love.
> Come fall awake.
> Come hold all of my cascading beauty
> my aching fragility.

Wild, uninhibited love is the single force powerful enough to send us head over heels, out of our minds and into our bodies; to bring us home to our senses. These enchantments ~ the same magic used by the flower who seduces a honey bee to carry pollen for his petalled love ~ hope to entice you to love the world in ways you have forgotten. *Carry this breath of devotion into the world....*

> To become bellows
> that blow the spark of love,
> kindling human hearts.
>
> To set ablaze a love-fire
> that burns out dead wood
> ~ domination, greed, exploitation ~
> and leaves fertilizing ash.
>
> To impregnate minds,
> and midwife the birthing
> of the *new*

To love the world is to walk the path of restoration and regeneration: a radical new-and-ancient relationship that sustains the *one-being* we have always been. And now we become again.

About this Book

After decades of teaching young children, several years ago I found myself with free time. I was inclined to gather a few friends here in my forest home; together we would explore the world of Sacred Ecology. I had been waiting years for this moment, and yet a quiet voice said "No. No human people yet. You must begin at the beginning. Go into the woods and encounter the *beings* who live there, your more-than-human neighbors. Go into *their* world; introduce yourself. They are far more aware of you than you imagine. They have been calling you."

I was taken aback, yet the words of Joy Harjo, America's Poet Laureate, echoed inside: "Remember the plants, trees, animal life who all have their families, their histories too. Talk to them, listen to them. They are alive poems."

Feeling clumsy, as if I had been sent to a foreign land with no idea of customs, no common language, no translator, no recognition of local foods, I simply began. Daily I walked quietly into the woods, apologizing for my unknowing, speaking the only language I know and listening with the ear of the heart. The consistent reply I received from the green world was *joy, joy, joy!* at being seen, honored, and spoken to. As days of listening have grown to months and years, secrets begin to open. These poems and meditations point toward the secrets, this *something* that is alive, a shared breath, a green blessing. I offer them to you, reader, in the following subtly nuanced ways:

~ *Litany is Invocation* calls by name the presences of animals, winds, plants, waters. It is a litany of wild saints. May you walk your own sacred places, calling their names, inviting relationship, giving gratitude.

~ *A Gaian Liturgy* is sacramental. Our gaze shifts from velvet moss underfoot and beech's copper leaves; it expands out to honor sweeping forces that shape all of life: woman-in-the-mountain, northern blue ice, the father of all incandescence. We bow to the four directions and the spiraling of time.

~ *Sacred Earth Sacred Self* recognizes the individual as an essential organism within the functioning of the whole. One's *self* is well and happy when held within the embrace of our people and our land; these guide us throughout our life. We are fertilized by light, gestated by breath; our ideas are carried on the breeze.

~ *Sacred Dreams* paints landscapes of the soul. These are shaped by the soul of the earth, Anima Mundi, whose deep currents form the archetypal riverbeds of Gaia herself. We become immersed in these mystic waters.

~ *Litany is Ceremony* asks us to gather friends, step outdoors, and hold hands. To become a circle of humanity embedded within the emerald circles that reach toward us and spiral into the cosmos.

I hope you will find this book to be like a deer path in the forest, perhaps barely perceptible to feet accustomed to traversing the built environment alone, yet enticing, veiled, beckoning. May these meditations invite you to open your heart, listen and reply. To allow yourself to be held and enfolded in a primordial mystery. To discover what lies beyond the first moist turn.

"What we need is a great, powerful, tremulous falling back in love with our old, ancient, primordial Beloved, which is the Earth herself."

MARTIN SHAW

Contents

"The tangible world itself is an iridescent sphere turning silently among the stars, a round mystery whose life is utterly eternal relative to ours, from out of whose vastness our momentary lives are born, and into whose vastness our lives recede, like waves on the surface of the sea.

An eternity we thought was elsewhere now calls out to us from every cleft in every stone, from every cloud and clump of dirt. To listen is to be turned inside out, discovering to our astonishment that the wholeness and holiness, the secret and sacred One we've been dreaming our way toward has been holding us all along, enfolding us in … unfathomable wholeness and complexity."

DAVID ABRAM, *Becoming Animal*

Introduction

It is January 2022. I look out into a quiet winter forest; pincushion and fern mosses are bright green in the forest's cold gray. In May I will search for wild showy orchids that cluster beside White Branch Creek. Mosses and orchids are good bio-indicators of healthy water, soil and air environments. Yet only a few hundred yards farther up the mountain oaks, poplars, hickory, and maple are being logged. We trade this complex web of living species and organisms ~ forests contain 80% of the world's bio-diversity ~ for pulpwood: Fourth of July paper plates and pellet stoves in China.

We are told we have ten years to find solutions, ten years to change the story.

How have we gone so wrong, and how do we begin to turn the tide? There are many things *to do,* ways to be involved. Paul Hawken's book *Drawdown,* for example, gives us 100 of the best ideas that can be put into practice right now, not only to stop carbon emissions, but also to re-sequester carbon back to a safe limit. If we can reduce carbon emissions to this level, it could give us time to develop the consciousness we need in order not simply to fix problems, but actually to *heal* the deadly mess our wrong-headedness has created.

A more hidden yet equally crucial question is *who can we become,* as a solution to this global crisis? Clearly, it is *who we are* as *human beings* that has put us, and our one home the earth, in this dangerous predicament. It is *who we are* that commits ecocide and therefore suicide. If we attempt to "fix the problems" from the same consciousness that has constellated the disaster, regardless of the good intentions, will any of these solutions turn the tide, or will they founder in wrong-thinking? Clearly, our paradigm of human domination is the root of these problems. It is important to explore how we have come to this deadly point in human consciousness. With this understanding, we will learn new and ancient ways of being human, in right relationship with all life. These will arc out in resonant fields and work in conjunction with all the good actions that must be done.

We ourselves must become new again; we need to envision a truly sustainable future for *all beings*. What is important is not simply what we do, but also *who we are* as we act.

We are shaped by the way we think; the nursery of thoughts is the collective human story, passed generation to generation. For the last many hundred years this has been a story of human ascendency: a story of our separation from the great round of Being. It is a story of shattered relationship, of domination, exploitation, and extraction. We witness the destruction and wreckage that has come as its logical result.

It is time for us to rediscover the primordial story of humanity's place in the cosmos. I believe it is crucial for us to retrace our steps, return to the place our human way of thinking diverged from the millennia-long-earth-story: that of symbiosis, cooperation, and collaboration. This organic form of growth has, through the miracles of synergy, evolved life from our single-celled ancestors to ever-higher, more multifaceted expressions of Being . We need to pick up the thread of this ancient story ~ still held by wisdom-keepers around the globe ~ make reparations for our wrongs, and step forward into a new chapter.

We do this by committing to the ageless principle of Oneness. By committing to the earth, Gaia herself, the one Being for whom all waters, landforms, winds, and species compose her living body, our home. We do this by finally acting on the realization that our astonishing and uniquely human way of thinking ~ our dazzling human brain ~ is given to us as a gift to be shared for the benefit of all life. The plains Indians' powerful greeting and prayer Mitakuye Oyasin, an affirmation that *All Beings Are Our Relatives*, carries this image of the great Circle of Life.

We will never recreate the past, and that should not be our intention. We must, anew, discover the *sacred earth* and humanity's sacred place within the Whole. We must find where and how we went wrong and act to return to balance: *We can be the homeopathic remedy for earth herself.* Our consciousness is the pathogen, yet it can become the remedy. According to Homeopathic Medicine's principles, a substance capable of *triggering* a certain disease can also be used to *treat* that disease. Let us explore and discover how we become the remedy.

Together let's pick up this thread of Oneness and explore through these meditations, dreams, and ceremony our biological-spiritual roots in the cosmos. Let's carry this thread of the sacred into the future. We can bring with us not only the traditional wisdom regained through right relationship with all beings, but also the rich treasures our new science offers. The ancient knowledge and new science can converge at this time as a fresh chapter arising within the very old love story of earth and cosmos. In collaboration with Gaia, we can help speak wholeness into being.

May the sensually alive images of this work ~ filled with the feelings, language, and joy of the animate earth ~ beckon and call us out of a 21st century numbing separation. Call us back to the Sacred Earth, and thereby help us perceive our Sacred Self. These meditations explore the sacred nature of earth in telluric landscapes alive with spirit and the personhood of all beings. We discover the human place in this inter-being through the principle of reciprocity ~ our fundamental kinship with all ~ as well as through the power of true speech, beauty, and love. We also find the sacredness of ourselves in more interior human landscapes: dreams, contemplations, imaginations. Perhaps you will experience these meditations as Earth's thoughts, moving through the world and through us in minerals, waters, warmth, wind.

My wish is that this litany of wild graces may enter you as a drink of fresh water, move through your liquid body, clear your mind, awaken your heart, seep into your dreams. In this way may you discover the place your next footstep falls and thereby help to shape the living future.

Litany is Invocation

Names have determined the world…We are made from words and stories, infinite chances through which we imagine ourselves.

KARENNE WOOD, MONACAN NATION, FROM *The Naming*

In the amber light of my childhood church I was mesmerized ~ held by the even pacing, the call and response. Bodies swayed and voices intoned Gregorian chant. Litanies of saints' names were called, their deeds and qualities remembered, their blessings called down as intercession for those of us still walking through life.

This practice of calling the names of ancestors to ask blessing and guidance ~ to ask for help ~ is a primary human cry. Australia's Aboriginal people walk the land, naming the Dreamtime ancestors who, in this way, remain present bringing power and abundance. The Haudenosaunee begin gatherings with long litanies that name and thank all beings, affirming unity with each repetition of "Now our minds are one"

What is this magic of *naming*? Of *calling forth*? Surely one part of the answer comes from the truth that we are shaped by sound. Our psyche and even our physical bodies are shaped differently when we walk beside the ocean's rolling waves and cry of sea birds than when in the din of the city's jackhammers and garbage trucks. When we say the names of our beloveds, the heart opens, eyes gleam, muscles soften.

Could it be that when we call the names of those who have gone before us, we draw open a veil between the seen and unseen worlds? We draw down their spirit to accompany us in the present moment. We "slide inside their skin" and know their wisdom from inside out. We humans, the "younger brother," are evolution's most recent progeny. We carry the long arc of Earth's evolution written into our DNA, architected into our bodies and sculpted in our brains. We held this collective wisdom for millennia, understanding intuitively that minerals and soil organisms, tall trees who call for rain and low fruiting ones, herd animals who fertilize prairies and predators who hold all in balance ~ we knew these were our elders, our teachers, our ancestors.

We now suffer a devastating amnesia, self-induced and deadly.

I walk my forest land listening for whispers of these other-than-human intelligences, calling a litany of their names as I pass ~ Garlic Mustard, Fiddlehead Fern, Beechnut, Curly Dock ~ naming their blessings. They entice me back to my senses, which carry the collective wisdom we have sadly lost. Step by step, they bring me back to the living breathing Earth, sensuously alive with our composite *Interbeing*. I invite you, the reader, to walk with me through these animate words. We will re-member, gather back into ourselves the scattered members of our wild foliated, feathered, finned, and furred family.

We will step outside the door, listen, and as we speak *ruby-throated hummingbird* our shoulders muscles will recall the mystical lemniscate of her wings. We will recite *honeysuckle blossom* and a heady, intoxicating sweetness will rise up within us. Our ears will open to many wild languages calling to us *come home*. Our skin will shuck off the tough husk of exploitation and extraction so our soft animal body can feel rain as grace, wind as god's breath, the taste of honey as love itself.

A Salute to Nations

when we become bees
we will know
self as sunlight
flowers

we will catch
bio-oscillations
~ the perception of others ~
ruffling through our wings

      in the green light of
      appalachian forests
      other-than-human
      nations convene for
            ceremony
            pageantry
            gift-giving
            prayer

      wild grapevine
      bows down
      to touch sacred earth

      troupes of
      translucent indian pipe
      are ceremonial
      ghost dancers

      proud mullein push
      new velvet leaves
      through leaf litter
      wear petal crowns

forest raspberry canes
are lavender flags
carried in late afternoon light

a republic of
   tubers
   seeds
   mushrooms
arrive from far away tribes
bringing gifts to give away

as bees bring sweet medicine
for all.

benevolence between species
~ our ancient heritage ~
will be a lived-understanding,
reality practiced body to body

at last we will come home
to the secret of love
hidden in the plain sight
of our own dna

Indian Pipe, monotropa uniflora, is a perennial wildflower. The entire plant is translucent, arising from the forest floor as luminous ivory. Emily Dickinson called Indian Pipe "the preferred flower of life." To encounter Indian Pipe is to see mystery made visible.

Dream Forest

Her feet walk
heart listens.
She wants to know
the way the worm knows
tunneling beneath his bark
through balsam dark
writing in a germinal hand.

Blind in his world of xylem
he makes poems
in her dreams
writes in wooden braille
tells of stardust
caught by trees
netted roots.

Each earthen word
becomes a point of light.
Star poems map fourteen
billion years
from now
to now,
written always
in this moment.

He measures evolution
in time filled with presence
time
      full
      fecund
      wild
round as the trunk

of the poplar
she stops beneath.

Round as tracings
she sees written
in bark
Round as all
she wants to know
beneath her feet
that walk and listen.

Animalia

I.
She hears a small thud
against the window.
Sparrow huddles,
breath coming fast,
blinks as the woman
bends to hold her.

No flutter of wings
quieter still
inside the basket.
The woman pulls
soft flannel close
steps back inside.

II.
Forest animals
she bows to by day
return to her
under moonlight.
They inhabit her dreams

> *She holds a wedding*
> *bouquet of living snakes*

> *Bees deposit honey*
> *into her lap*

> *Birdsong becomes*
> *elixir in a crystal vial*

A stag with diamond antlers
stands in shallow creek water

Her house of dreams
is a living bestiary
   herds, packs, flocks, schools
   species, times, seasons, eons
   are waves on the sea
   rising, merging, rearranging
   patterns of furred, finned
    feathered bodies
   surfacing and receding

III.
When humans stood to walk
face forward, gaze level
the underside
~ belly, womb, heart ~
were exposed
vulnerable for the first time.

Rolling over
wolves submit
with a lowered head
tail tucked
underbelly soft and visible.

The woman rounds
her body, bends low
forehead on the ground
to bow bare
before the Sacred.

IV.
One sparrow
the weight of feathers
and a heartbeat
launches into flight
from a basket rim.

Wild Cathedrals

Light-eating spirits,
flora are ancestral forces.
Photosynthesizing,
they make divinity
visible to our blunt human sight:

> *Beech trees open their*
> *copper arms*
> *touch hair*
> *greet and bless.*
> *Silvery glade ferns bow,*
> *exude antediluvian perfume.*
> *Curling grapevine tendrils swing*
> *in the wind of our passing.*

The central flame,
the green light, rooted
ever-rising
is the mitochondrial matrix.
Its combustive heat
fed by pacifist chloroplasts
turns stardust into flesh:

> *Damsel-fly snaps open*
> *peacock green wings*
> *she is an elegant*
> *kabuki dancer*
> *suspended in flight*
> *above the creek.*
> *Bear cub strolls the path*
> *a granddaughter walked last eve.*

Coyote's signature is written in
morning's creek-side mud.

The still point
~ empty core of life's axis ~
is the central beam
of wild cathedrals.
It holds up the night sky
to become evening's
intimate roof

the only dome
vast enough to carry
human dreams.

Let us recognize plants as our living ancestors, photosynthesis as divine activity, the
still point as god's inhalation.

Night Breath

In nuanced darkness
the spherical nature of sound
echoes in cochlear spirals.

Cicada's song resonates
with red fox's shrill bark
and moonlit breezes.

Through tapestried shadows
the breath repeats *Huuuu...*
heart beating its rhythm.

This breath, created by
tulip poplars and spice bush,
we share with

>   red-winged blackbirds
>   who feed their fledgling
>   one sunflower seed by one
>
>   orcas breaching and
>   shimmering in sunlight
>   as they play off Vashon Island
>
>   a bob cat whose shriek
>   punctuates
>   pungent dark.

It is a layered elixir infused with
the exhaled dreams of boundless
furred and feathered ancestors

since the first chloroplast
invited mitochondria to dance
a tango of symbiosis.

Each breath, a stratified
sedimentation of beings
a fertile broth

drifts damp and lush
through bedroom windows.

The Speaking Earth

Sound is a formative force: we are shaped by what we hear. Our ancient primate ancestors lived bathed in sounds, the language of a vibrant fecund new earth busy with love's work of evolution. We first learned to speak by listening to the musical language that surrounded us, the living intelligence it conveyed. The whistling of wind through red rock canyons, the call and response of crashing waves and sand susurration, the intricately accurate newscasting systems of bird language. We also heard stones speak silently as they broadcast their electromagnetic fields into soil and water. Their minerals still speak in our bloodstream as health and vibrancy: our well-being falters without mineral language. Plant dialogue tells of nutrition, medicine, pleasure.

We grew up in this river of language, and out of this our human speech arose to naturally imitate and reflect the life-force that sounded all about us. Our original languages were expressive of broad sense perception, wide expanses of movement, of nuanced felt-experiences in this sensuous earth; they were languages of verbs. The native Potawatomi language even today contains seventy percent verbs. As we live further removed from the wild, living earth we recede further into mental *conceptions* of the world. More and more removed from our wild and sensuous selves, we find our language today composed of seventy percent nouns. Verbs tell us about the activities of beings; nouns name things. Having devalued the *being-ness* of earth ancestors, we now live in a small perceptual prison this narrowing of language both reflects and perpetuates.

Other voices speak of other kinds of intelligences. Enter into these invocations; listen with me. Let's allow these other ways of knowing to rise up through the bottom of our feet and send mycellial networks' delicate strands of mind through our pores. Allow earth-knowing to percolate up through our strata; it is fresh groundwater bringing life to barren thought. Perhaps our moistened words will grow wings and spiral upward on warm currents or grow foliated and plentiful, reaching into arid regions of mind to seed the clouds of thought and call sweet rain.

"The written word carries a pivotal magic – the same magic that once sparkled for us in the eye of an owl or the glide of an otter. Let us release the budded, earthly intelligence of our words, freeing them to respond to the speech of the things and beings themselves, to the green uttering forth of leaves from the spring branches. Let us find phrases that place us in contact with the trembling neck-muscles of a deer holding its antlers high as it swims toward the mainland.. Let us plant words like seeds, under rocks and fallen logs, letting language take root, once again, in the earthen silence of shadow and bone and leaf."

DAVID ABRAM

Word

I.
The world
pregnant with language,
thoughts were carried
as heartbeat and breath
~ feral knowing ~
by scent,
a slight breeze
ruffling feather and fur.

Language rumbled up alive
hiccupped out in mirth
whistled high pitched
and nasal in warning,
cooed in need,
keened in sorrow,
carried in bio-chemistry and
synaptic electricity.

II
When we birthed
human words
they were beings.
Alive, sacred
they shaped the world.
Filled with intelligence of
weight, volume
fingertips in sand
soft belly or
flexed knee
full of vision
and dream

words were always verbs
enfolded in primal activity
ever becoming
            unfurling
            exchanging
            luminescing

Words were children
of an animate earth:
electrons flashing
in and out of orbit
strands of DNA spiraling
coding for existence
stones broadcasting
electromagnetic voices.

Words born
of wind-sculpted
red rock bluffs
of warmth bubbling up
from volcanic springs,
they instructed
a new naked
creature: vulnerable,
eyes shining with
new light.

III
When we chained words
made them slaves of concept
they became nouns.
We lost our way.
Words livingness denied,
we exclude ourselves
from conversations
            quacked

                    growled
                    whistled
                    honked.
We no longer twine
in creative passion
with a breathing
emerging earth.
Humans behind screens
we hold words behind bars
reduce life to *things*
declaring we alone
have voice and
agency.

IV
Reimagine words:

Listen for meaning and mood
as wind rustles dry grass
and mice rattle seed-heads.

Understand the beat of wings;
dawn geese rise
from mist-laden pond.

Now land will sculpt mind
as water carves
sandstone canyons.

Mind
listening to coyote song
and owl speech
will sprout
softly velvet new antlers
or become
a chambered nautilus.

Know the way out
is the way in:
    retrace recent steps
    return to
    where-we-went-wrong
    make reparations
so our words
our stories
can return to
the great conversation
among elements
and beings.

Together as one
we will sing the world alive.
Again.

Mountain Speech

Walk inside mountains.
Intimately merged,
a babe in womb,
blood rhythm set by
mountain breath,
mountain's pace.

Tectonic plates push;
glacial ice polishes.
One stone at a time
thrusts up against feet.
Ligament, muscle, hip
move to make room for

>mountain ore,
>mountain thought,
>mountain speech.

Learn Gaia's timeless alphabet,
the dialect of alabaster, basalt, granite.
Know the stories told in star nurseries.
Speak the language of comet-born light
that comes to rest
in mountain's crystalline syllables.

Jack-in-the-Pulpit

Ideas, siloed like wheat
that is lifted out of native soil,
away from the microbes
who make bread into flesh
~ ideas exiled in sterile
towers of thought ~
tethered to the desk,
she writes.

     All the while
     in pungent
     pine-carpeted forest
     amid hickory
          poplar
          wild cherry
     birds sing evensong.
     Cicadas are Tibetan monks
     droning intoning.
     Forest's persistent
     emerald light calls out
     an invitation.
     She accepts.

     Eyes flooded
     with rippling green
     orienting by touch
     a thrill raises
     tiny hairs on her
     bare arms.
     There stands
     Jack-in-the-Pulpit,
     a head taller than

humble moss and creepers.

She listens to
his wild sermon:
"We are God's thoughts:
we travel through
chemical collaborations
        enzymes
        proteins
        sugars.
We are the sustainers
        cycling
        enfolding
        harnessing nourishment
offering the forest's bread:
        oyster mushroom
        poplar's tulip
        wine berry
        paw-paw
        hazelnut
We are holy ideas-in-motion."

Now indoors
vital thought forces
come surging from her pen.
Like lightning
they catalyze spirit,
pump life-blood
into concepts
too long preserved
in the salt of separation.

They bring new words
to roam across the page
like migratory herds.

Or are they starlings
flying in perfect unison
to sing the mind awake?

Jack-in-the Pulpit is a shade loving wildflower found in moist deciduous woods like mine. Its exotic flower, on an elegant tall stalk, is green and maroon; it is a show-stopper on a woodland walk.

Remedy

Write.
To mend the hole in the world
to summon pages that
chatter
      hoot
           bark
                honk.
To craft
image
      texture
           landscape
               wingbeat

To make a wild call
seduce the narcissistic mind
dislodge our posturing hubris
our pride born when we stole words from
rock face
      thunderstorm
           desert sage
              balsam fir

and held their voices prisoner on the bare page
until our self involved shouts and protests
have deafened the human ear
and we no longer
hear voices
antlered
      furred
           four-legged
             taloned

Write, instead,
language embedded in land
words pronounced by other than human
presences
      gestures
           resonance
                intelligence

Cicada's muscular thrum
braided through
with cricket's
sparkling song

bright and measured
cricket-cadence persists
when autumn leaves drift
to become November's
final refrain
and winter silence descends.

Honey-combed mountain springs
gurgle shyly
into freshet's tumbled murmur
merging into streamlets' songs
feeding the chorused voice
of White Branch Creek.

Yet the wood thrush's polyphonic serenade
becomes a requiem for forests.
Saws drone while
hickory,
      beech
           poplar
                oak

tumble
to become pellet fuel
for stoves in China.

Write.
To hear the original voices
to remember our place in the One
to mend the hole in the world.

In an Ancient Tongue

Under leaf litter,
a lace web:
mycelial language
hurries across

    stones
    roots
    tubers.

Arcs across

    poplar and spicebush
    hickory and beech
    walnut and cherry

It tells of

    triage
    nutrition
    water

Human fingers become
transparent threads
learn the fungal vernacular
know the slang for

    minerals
    sunlight
    photosynthesis

Fingers touch
subtle infrastructure

listen to hear
the syllables for

      mist
      configuring pools
      at poplar's root.

To Know

Forest beings teach:
See spirit
joined with landscapes
of visible light
radiating pure
from solar visage.
Apprehend ambient reflections
echoing back from
rock face.
Learn to speak the
vocabulary of rooted
tellurian gods.

Unseen beings ask:
See spirit in
uncreated light,
in luminous dark.
See resonant spheres in
nesting universes,
beyond vision's spectrum
past the
boundaries of mind.
Speak the dialect of the ethers,
a silent language that rides
the currents of breath.

Sacred Time

We have broken the golden round of time, imprisoned its magic pliancy inside our harsh measurement. With our precise hammers we have hacked its wholeness into ever-smaller fractions. Past is imprisoned behind us and futures walk before us wielding whips. Believing we have conquered time, we now discover who is master, as our technology drives us relentlessly toward a future we can never reach.

Yet time, in essence, is an organic being who sings to us of morning's star, moonlight in a velvet sky, and the symphony of seasons. It is cousin to heartbeat and footstep. The qualities of love ~ joy in sensory enchantment, visceral pleasures in rhythmic work, the shelter of belonging to a vast family of being ~ these arise in the presence of the *eternal now*. Past and future accompany us moment by moment throughout our days.

The past is present now directly beneath our feet, as the geological and oceanographic practices of taking core samples demonstrate. Ancient peoples knew the past is always present, and believed the future is held in our hands and minds, as well. Even today Sufis invoke litanies, the beautiful qualities of the divine, bringing them from infinite possibilities into breath and form, creating futures in this moment, the next, and next...

Step with me through these green fields. Let us align ourselves with the beauty that is spread out before our eyes *now*; know that beauty supports us from the past and calls to us from unimaginable futures. The thirteenth-century poet Rumi urges us: "Let the beauty we love be what we do. There are hundreds of ways to kneel and kiss the ground"*

We will walk together, you and I. We will bow.

From Jelalludin Rumi, beloved thirteenth century Sufi mystic and poet

Pursuit

April
Court the poplar
at water's confluence:

    Speak the original language
    song, prayer, offerings
    wrapped in leaves.

    Listen to arboreal speech.
    Slip inside the bark
    veins become phloem.

    Woman inside the wood
    enchanted
    is a wind harp.

July
Woo the waters:

    Fingers trail amid
    crayfish
    minnows
    flat green stones.

    Caress sand and silt;
    they are twin sisters

        Star shine glitters in
        pre-eternal sand.
        Carbon's combustive cycle
        deposits silk-spun silt.

Electromagnetic signatures
are written in an elegant hand

    sand: *tourmaline*
      jasper

    silt: *nitrogen*
      hydrogen

October
  Propose to crickets:

    Their song pulses
    on a heartbeat
    echoes in cochlear spirals
    steadies the breath.

    Crickets are winter's Persephone.
    Too soon gone,
    they grace the underworld.

January
  Wed earth's timeless round:
    January's silence cries
    till frozen crystals fall
    from opaque skies

    and cardinals shine
    as drops of blood
    on a bridal hillside.

Equinox

Celestial geometry
maps star voyages
that navigate cosmic seas.

One beam of earth's star
rays out low across land,
glances off stones
standing at sunset.

Now a telluric ritual begins
      October Lady's Tresses
      ~floral spears~
      point to summer's
      final hours.

      Lobelia wears a violet crown:
      medicine for breath
      and dreams.

      Frost grapes and porcelain berries
      shine plump, heavy,
      tempt autumn's fox.

Witness earth's weight shift
as she moves toward quiet,
toward her fragrant rite
      laying down
      layering up
      mounded, umber
            oak and poplar leaves
            bee balm flower stalks
            beds of bracken.

This is her ceremony of soil;
magic at its most potent.
Winter's death is a chrysalis
returning to its
embryonic state.

Fluid with possibility
~ pluripotent ~
earth turns toward sleep.

Invocation

Walk
at the center of
time and space
cosmic dust steady
beneath our feet
as segmented worms
tunnel.
Ancient ones
　　　fossils
　　　mineral strata
　　　bones of
　　　great grandparents
carry us.

Listen to language
of an earthly cosmology.
World-soul speaks
　　　as breezes rattle bamboo

　　　as wood-thrush's complex
　　　refrain echoes

　　　and voices of
　　　rain, rivers
　　　ocean currents
　　　sing in our veins

Children not yet born
call from unseen realms.
Unimaginable futures
beckon to us.
Galaxies converge as

we set each foot on
sacred ground.

Gather not only the past
   all-that-has-been,
cast a net, as well, into the vast
   all-that-can-be.

Call down
Call here
Bring forward

protection
     corridors of light

sustenance
     needs met by grace

guidance
     navigation by soul- light

a clear path
     obstacles removed by unseen hands

Past
future
here
everywhere
human
other-than-human
congregate.

With
    this footstep
    now this
call the future.

Come.

Many Native cultures around the world, and physicists as well, do not separate time and space, but see them as a functioning continuum. The past is present all around us, directly beneath our feet. And the future is present in the subtle atmosphere right here and now, waiting to be called-in. It is our human responsibility to choose our thoughts, words and actions wisely, for they call-forth the future.

Indigenous

I.
Moccasined feet tread
soft on forest
leaf-litter.

Greeting sacred stones with
song and prayer
bringing
ceremony
for spirits of the
spring, the girl bends to drink.

Water rises through
mineral strata
its voice
sings
an everlasting
story. She drinks

as her people have, since
Beginning Time.
Poplars
fine-
skinned, guard
this sacred spring.

Spice bush gathers close.
Water cress rings
its basin.
Shepherd's purse
shakes heart-shaped
pods in a spring breeze.

II.
Four centuries pass:
        Stolen land
        Stolen children
        Stolen lives
Destroyed
        Language
        Song
        Ceremony

A litany of suffering
too vast for mouths to speak.

Her people persist,
yet the mill
now claims this
native land.

III.
That day it was my footfall
in the fragrant woods.
Surprised when
the logger
arrived
I offered him
friendship, conversation. I

pointed toward the moist glade
asked for his care,
hoped
that looking
into his eyes
would protect her spring.

I should have become
a quail hen,

run
limping
feigning a broken
wing, thrown my body

between the predator and the nest.

> IV.
> Machinery is gone; gravel
> oppresses forest loam;
> motor oil pools in
> sinister rainbows
> with each rainfall.
>
> Forester's blue ribbon proclaiming
> *"Water Present. Stay Clear"* is
> ground to bits
> in bulldozer tire tracks.
>
>
> Poplar's infinite grace
> is now processed
> into board-feet.
> Raw stumps ache
>
> in the hot sun.
> Encircling stones
> scattered. Wind
> ~ breath of Spirit ~
>
> tells the forest's
> sorrow. Broken trees
> cry out and gesture,
> arms thrown high in grief.

Wind calls to four
directions, asking
    Look here,
    see this
    witness all
    bring prayers.

V.
I try to listen, the way she did
before the archaeology
of devastation:

listen
to the voices of
the water and land.

I write the words of water's
story, as November's
umber leaves
hurry across
the shoulders of these
ancient springtime mountains.

They tell of tragedy
    the forest's siege
    their fallen mothers
    the mycelium's silence.

Yet, mountain speaks
resilience, too:
    spicebush makes triage
     ~ a poultice for fresh scars ~
      its "first green is gold."

young red maples open
their blossoms; they wear
fringed crimson skirts

quartz crystals pure as ice
push up between the toes
of poplar stumps

cloven hoof prints
appear in logging road
tire tracks

turkey scratch
rearranges
logging slash.

VI.
Remembering native elders
and the timeless girl at
the spring, I bring

a child
of five years. We
sing offerings and prayers

we gather spring greens. I recite
their names: a different
litany

now: that
of wild saints. She repeats:

Shepherd's purse
Cleavers
Chick weed

            Wild Onion
         Garlic mustard
      Watercress.

Green words of resurrection,
resilience. The mountain and
her people are
still here.

This is a "shape poem," in which the shape of the words reflect that which is being described. Parts I, III and V are shaped like waves lapping the spring's edge and leaves dancing in the mountain wind. Parts II and IV are harshly linear, measured and controlled, reflecting Pope Alexander's brutal Papal Bull "The Doctrine of Discovery" decreed in 1493. This became the basis of all European claims in the Americas, and the genocide of the Native American people.

Sacred Place

We have desecrated *sacred place*. Having stolen *place's* breath and spirit, we deem it empty space, no longer teeming with presences seen and unseen, with ancestors and heirs. Imagining it inert, we subject it to quantification, with monetization always close behind. The commons ~ our birthright to be in living relationship with waters, lands, food plants, shade trees, fishes, fowl, four-leggeds ~ is stolen, carved into sections, bought and sold. Its life-spirit, desacralized as resources, is extracted and put on the market to the highest bidder.

Yet *sacred place* is our original home, nuanced within folds of forested hillsides each unique with sun-spangled oak or hickory, fern and pin cushion moss, or meadows thronging with asters and goldenrod, stately mullein guarding roadsides; each place radiating its particular scent of spirit.

Let us reclaim our human heritage as keepers of the land, lovers of *this* particular tulip poplar with her five silver trunks and emerald moss growing on the north side, become kin to stream bed stones carrying *these* effulgent waters that flow over them. We are heirs to the wisdom of unseen ancestors who crowd close as we make offerings and prayers; partners to other-than-human beings who perceive us as clearly as we perceive them; benefactors to countless generations, descendants who watch our actions with bright hope.

To Come Home

Empty space
       stolen child
       of Place
       of home
is an extracted thing
a wraith without
heartbeat or flesh.

The howling winds
of desolation
blow through
such emptiness:
       the human mind
       unmoored from
       heart-spirit-land
       imagines itself
       alone
       in an empty world.

This lonely child
bereft of the fertile
place-between:
without relationship

       of river bank
       and raccoons catching crawfish

       of seashore
       and pelicans fishing at dusk

       of wild beehives
       and winged honeyguides

this child of air, breath of spirit
child of *the teeming unseen*
            weeps with longing.
            Her tears rain
            inside my body

and so I walk redemption.

Now this foot I set
upon holy soil
now this one
upon star moss
now sand beside
the sacred stream
now the tenderness of
sweet clover.

The blessed scent
of leaf mold exudes
as feet caress
and empty space
comes home
to fullness
to *Place*.

The expression "stolen child of Place" refers to generations of Indigenous Australian children who were removed from their families by Federal and State government agencies and church missions. The "place between" refers to the understanding that what we in the West refer to as empty space, is actually never empty: it is teeming with Dreamtime Ancestors, with story and song lines, it is eternally creative and most importantly, relational. Traditional Aboriginal art portrays what we call "background" filled with hatch marks. This brings it to foreground and honors the invisible relationships that surround us.

Wild Showy Orchids

It is autumn
in the time
of climate change.
She feels
the rip-tide swirl
pulling life into the bottleneck

as loggers turn
her mountain forests
into pulp and
fourth of July
paper plates.

She walks her prayers
feet press them
into fragrant loam.
By winter
her body
is a talisman

      a poultice
      for open wounds
      an amulet
      for protection.

She paces
now this
wooded path
now that.

Come May, prayers
germinate

beneath her feet
send out broad
glossy leaves.

Stalks arise
graceful as swan's necks.

      Wild orchids open
      fuchsia throats
      sip grace
      which falls
      as rain.

Prayer for the Salmon Nation

Water protectors sing
drums speak.
Prayers rise with sage smoke
invite convocation.

Throngs seen and unseen call
Water is Life.
Ancestors dance
footsteps call out prayers.

Spirit languages arise
like incense from
      forests
      prairies
      mountains
      winds
      waters.

Ancestors cry warnings:

      waters given when
      the world was new
      speak in plain terms
          epic floods
          hurricane rain
          tsunamis
          poisoned water

      fire spells danger
      in tongues of flame
          heat waves
          drought

        desiccated croplands
        deserts marching

    arboreal spirits rise within humans
    cycles
    seasons
    seeds
    bloom in our bodies
    fruit in human psyche
    while forests fall.

Join bird nations
feathers in the hair;
join animal relatives
with furs on ochre bodies.

Ghost dancers leading,
sing unity.
Feet beating rhythm,
pray as one.

Lift one thread of
life's fabric ~
        the whole
        tapestry moves.

Lift up this thread
for the Salmon Nation:
invisible hosts
dance prayer in circles.
Act to protect:
Water is Life.

No fracked gas in
the Salish Sea

not in the home
of the Salmon People.

> *dance with elders*
> *follow original instructions*
> *learn by grace.*

Or learn by carnage.

The choice is ours to make.

The Ghost Dance evolved as a ceremony associated with the Native American prophecy of an end to white expansion, and encouraged cross-cultural cooperation and non-violence among tribes. "Prayer for the Salmon Nation" was inspired by the ongoing efforts of the Puyallup Tribe and other Washington State Tribes who have always called themselves the Salmon People, and know the salmon in the Salish Sea are their ancestors. Their work to save the salmon creates positive ecological changes throughout the entire region.

Honey Bee

April sun's warm vortex
carries her up
ever up.
Suitors spiral higher
toward her lucent flight.
Entwined, they dance
penetrated by light.

She brings devotion's glow
into her hive; feeds it
to each daughter
who works
among the flowers
making drops of love
into honey.

Her pearlescent eggs
are spiraling stars
in an apian Milky Way.
She lays them
in hexagonal cradles
while hot southern sun
permeates
her cosmos.

She carries sun mysteries
inside her body
while honey heralds
bees and land
as one.

> *The Queen Bee lays her golden eggs in cosmic patterns that spiral throughout the bee-hive.*

Generate

This is dance. Play.
The elemental table.
It is crystallized form.

The color of water.
Empty. Full.
This is the causal force.

> Cumulus and stratus
> are air-borne oceans.

> Teal waters
> touch volcanic sands.

> One white crane glides
> through bamboo waves.

> Generating and generated.
> Blessing and blest.

Tectonic plates push mountains.
Entropy grinds sand.
Carbon begets biology.

Earth. Water. Fire. Air.
Dervishes all,
they whirl at the

doorway between the worlds,
turning ever toward
The Heart.

Love Beauty

Choose Beauty, tend it, protect it

Dig deep, through all the layers of ecosystem destruction: carbon emissions, pesticide poisoning, mining, clear-cutting, fracking, cascading species loss, bee colony collapse, drought, flood, famine. The world of human enterprise is built on pillars of domination, exploitation and extraction. Denying the *personhood* of the land, waters, plants, animals ~ denying they are our elders, our relatives ~ in this way we turn our hearts to stone. We lose our humanity. Declaring selfhood and agency belong to us alone, we insist other-than-human people are *things* and in this way we excuse our enslavement of them. Is it a surprise that we also enslave ourselves, other human beings, black, brown, native? We witness the obvious, logical conclusion ~ a world devastated, pillaged , weeping for mercy.

The most radical act we can make is to step with our vulnerable bodies into the suffering world. Look around; see the contempt of beauty, witness the destruction that necessarily follows. Allow deep grief to sweep through us, wash over us wave upon wave, scour clean our inertia, scrub away the lies we have been taught. Our only hope is to let the sorrow transform us and bring us to love. Let love school us, reshape our seeing, hone our listening, finely tool our feelings.

Love is the answer. It is the only power strong enough to break these chains of exploitation and extraction with which we violate our beautiful home, planet earth. Love is the first footstep along a new path; we can find this new way by love's light alone. Love will inform and shape our actions. It will be the fulcrum of every decision we make. Love will restore beauty and through this we can uncover our own buried humanity. We can regain our small place in the great circle of life.

Let us allow these words to seduce us back toward love, toward beauty, toward our true selves. We begin now in this spacious, pregnant moment.

"May Truth be your pen and Love your ink. Always write Love with Love"
SHEIKH TAPDUK EMRE, 13TH CENTURY TEACHER OF
MYSTIC POET YUNUS EMRE

The Generosity of Moss

Neural meaning-structures evolve.
Mind dethroned
we now shape energy
with heart.
A soil organism feels
through pregnant dark
the generosity
of moss and lichen
sightless
perceives this nutrition
as gift.

Sheer impetus of touch
engenders knowledge.
We too can perceive
by daylight
arenas of subtlety

that come to us
by radiant dark.
Shaping energy
with bell-like clarity
resonant fields
become a flower mandala

in the more-than-visible world.
Meaning inheres
in each petal
reweaving the rip
in the world.

"Neural meaning-structures evolve." We can experience this more ancient way of
knowing as we allow our consciousness to drop from our heads deeper down into our
original organ of perception, the heart. The electro-magnetic waves created by the
oscillations of the heart emanate outward and impact the world around us through
entrainment, thereby "shaping energy."

Effaced

cascading leaves are
emerald waves
on an afternoon breeze

each shade of green
sings itself
in a foliate sea

walk
drawn into
verdant depths

fall into
unbounded detail

       perfumed loam
       feather moss
       dove's song

merge with

       fungal strands
       all healing ginseng
       chanterelle mushrooms

breathe in symbiosis with

       emerald beingness
       communal singularity
       pregnant wildwoods

disappear into fecund alchemy

Ice Caps

Folding linen napkins
embroidered pears in corners
the ones used on father's day

    coleslaw, baked beans
    children, grandchildren
    parents, cousins
    love and pathos

she listens.

The sound of a
polar ice cap melting
is sweet
this June evening.
Arctic ice falls
as summer rain

onto the kitchen garden
birds sing
exhaling forest scents
prehistoric ferns grow
to Pangean proportions.

The old cat is
dying of infected toenails.
The urgency of the present moment
tiny and alterable
begs attention

    apply antibiotic
    between toes daily

fold laundry
love grandchildren
pray.

This is the place
she *can* touch
have impact.

Farther north, Inuit families
pack their lives in boxes

can of coffee
ivory figurines
carved from walrus tusks
transistor radio
ceremonial drum.

They move their
village higher inland.
Those poorer
can only watch
as ice melts.

A hungry polar bear
swims through
open seas
no walruses
in sight.

All the while geologic time
        moving ever in the present
drops slow rain
on a cool Virginia evening
as she weeps
for the places
she *cannot* touch.

About Darwin

Darwin knew half.
Gaia's knowing is whole.

>Outright aggression
>ushers in resonant fields
>of cooperation.

>Light-eating chloroplasts
>become bellows
>for mitochondrial fires.

>A green ocean of trees
>a tidal wave of humans
>we breathe in symbiotic harmony.

>Photosynthesis and respiration
>eternally twined
>in a lover's embrace.

Wildness
encoded in every living cell
is not all tooth and claw.

>Owl shrills in
>cold moonlight.
>The rabbit in me

>~ ten thousand
>lives lived as prey ~
>trembles.

Yet by morning's light
maidenhair ferns unfurl
green galaxies.

Trillium opens
a foliated holy trinity.
Jack-in-the-Pulpit
preaches from deepening shade.

To understand the science behind "Outright aggression ushers in resonant fields of cooperation. Light-eating chloroplasts become bellows for mitochondrial fires" read Earth Dance: Living Systems by Elisabet Sahtouris.

Original Instructions

Unlike units that march
in formation through
technology-soaked heads
wild thought patterns
are *fluid-knowing*.

Spirit slips through capillaries of mind
       seeps across equatorial deltas
       migrates with tidal salt marshes.

Each molecule
steeped in spirit's honeyed
vibrant plasma
is held in
dynamic equipoise.
Unseen, vast fields of being
participate.

Palpable visible partners
share this knowing, too:
       starlight
       Antarctic ice
       cacao groves
       savanna lions
       orca whales.

To design sacred space,
form is molded
by thoughts and gestures of
the world soul.

Humans offer
the currents of a natural mind

if we follow the
original instructions.

Birth Canal

Human concepts are
seeded by epochs of boundless
evolving forms;
each being conceives knowledge
in the body,
gestates it
as felt experience.

The blood of thought flows
through cycling millennia;
is scaffolded in sinew and bone
choreographed into
an exquisite unitive matrix:
the ever evolving mind,
our intelligent, perceiving heart.

A Gaian Liturgy

There is One Holy Book, the sacred manuscript of nature,
the only scripture which can enlighten the reader.

HAZRAT INAYT KHAN

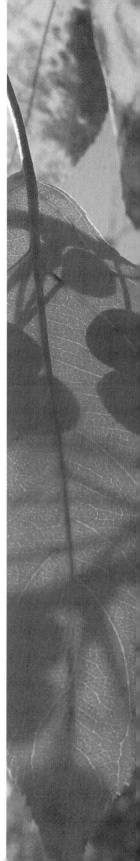

To Reimagine Liturgy

Gaia's own liturgy offers the possibility that we be released from the binding structures of the Western mind. A new liturgy and its rituals can blur the edges of our sense of self and open the door to unitary states: unite the boundlessness of Spirit with the eternally cycling here and now.

Gaian liturgy is sacramental: outward and visible realities express the subtle movements of Spirit. The unfurling of springtime's fiddlehead fern announces the sacred miracle of Spirit's seed, as it unfolds not only in the green world, but also in the sacrament of our own bodies. The tangible and finite make Spirit visible. This liturgy offers us a communal lens through which to witness such truth. With spoken rhythms and gestures, scriptures and texts, prayer's call and response, the human community is woven together for a sacred *moment outside of time* into one body, one heart, one mind. We become one living expression of praise, in communion with all beings. The resonant states created by a participatory liturgy lift us out of isolation, unbind us from the narrow confines of solitary thought. We become embedded in something greater than ourselves, a pervasive joyous intelligence that

> leaps branch to branch
> tunnels in the dark
> bursts open perfumed buds
> osmoses cell walls
>
> fuses particles and births stars
> collapsing them as black holes
> into which time-space
> the laws of physics and
> all our collective hubris
> disappear.

In these invocations we return to a liturgy of the incarnate deity . Let us gather friends and family, and together experience these healing, unitive states. Let them be written into our bloodstream, carried in the rhythm of our footsteps. Let us walk this ecstatic unity into the moments of our daily lives.

Let us begin now.

Gratitude to all Beings

Mineral

Minerals are stardust
coalesced in deep space
messengers of light shot
from Sagittarius' bow.
Luminous arrows travel through
a new sun's orbit.
Pulled by love's gravity
they shape the intelligence of light
into Appalachia's igneous core.
Electromagnetic signatures ray
invisibly from caves' palpable dark.

Woman-in-mountain is our sister
breasts twin peaks
waist a deep valley
hips rising smooth
long thigh bone
a treeless ridge.

Her timeless gaze
illumines evening's blue ridge.
Her minerals tumble
through our blood
like stones
carried in highland freshets
come to rest for a time
in our shoulder blades, ribs

then flow on
to nourish sacred ground.

Each poem appears on a separate page, giving you, reader, air and light; time to
breathe and experience your own ritual of thanks.

Minerals are children of light, flung into space at each star's birth.

Water

Water beings arrive as
pure benediction.
Ice diamonds fall through
interstellar space, drift
into earth's warm breath
to become mist
hovering above
river's slow elbow.
Translucent curtains of rain
billow in valley breezes.

Drops sipped from
cupped hands
will flow differently, now,
eddying among veins
osmosing cell walls
hydrating neural highways.
Particles of human thought
will flow out to soil organisms
migrate into Ivy Creek
eager to find the sea
      be pummeled by surf
      pause in tidal pools
      before becoming
      northern blue ice
      an Inuit kayak
      paddling close.

Plant

Rivanna river bank
damp earth a fecund womb
gestates plant embryos

who dream of water
          grace fallen from stars
who ache toward sun's warmth
          his sovereign ascendency.

Plant ancestors live
through our cycles
moon to moon
          blossoming
          fruiting
          seeding
          resting
We are kin
to seductive honeysuckle
          unfurling first leaves
          opening blossom's
          fertile whorl into
          crimson dawn light
kin to masting beech trees
          sisters, cousins
          who together as one
          launch their precious
          young, making forests
          fill with music:
          nuts cascading
          from upper stories
          squirrels gathering
          gossiping amid leaf litter

kin to blackberries who open
      their taut, sweet fruit
      into lustrous solar face

Beech trees do not fruit yearly or biennially. By a mysterious communication, beeches
in an entire bio-region will set, mature and launch their fruit at the same time:
mast-fruiting.

Animal

Wide cretaceous wingspan
heron descends in majesty
steps high
with ancient grace
through autumn's garden stream.
Cool intense gaze
studies creek-bank
stream bed
plucks a
crayfish midstream
> an elegant Asian woman
> she reaches with chopsticks
> to extract a plump water chestnut.
Woman moored at the window
a slight quiver trembles between
shoulder blades
as bird ascends
cruising
with slow deep wing beats.

Coyote prints in mud
bear scat amid birdseed
possum's marsupial parenthood:
we bow to
their warm blood
salute the sun-being
who walks across
his blue arch
raying out beneficence
generosity.
The father of all incandescence
brings light

by the gift of fire.
Our limbs are warm
hearts ablaze
free.

Light

Fire's incandescence dies
into silk. Albedo. Ash.
Cool, nutritious
alabastrine as spider's web
it sweetens acid soil
warms with a tender hand:
   destruction eclipsed
   by grace.

Ash, nutrient rich,
dug back into human soil
alkalizes
phosphorizes
bio-luminesces.
No longer making
light by heat
we metamorphose.
Now
   our lucid prayers
   and conversations
   with glowing fungi

are coronas of light
in the dazzling dark:
   we become
   the communion
   of light upon light.

The phrase "light upon light" refers to the Qur'anic Verse of Light or Ayat-al-Nur, which begins "Allah is the light of the heavens and the earth." Most light is created by a process of combustion, by heat. Bioluminescence on the other hand, occurs in the interaction ~ the relationship ~ between electrons and photons. Our light-filled prayers to the heavens and our lucid relationships with earth-beings are reflections of the ongoing cosmic and telluric love affair.

Air

We grow translucent
with imprint of wind.
Conjoined Spirit
      composed of god's breath and
      signatures of animal kin
opens our gills-become-lungs.
Oxygen cycles
through geologic time
through an elongated
history of evolving bodies'
animate tissue.
Breath is a tender sharing
honed through millennia
      coevolved with conifers
      tree frogs, great blue heron
      black bear mothers
      wind rushing down canyons.

Vapor, breeze, gust, zephyr:
living air
lived inter-being.
To be a gnat in this
amaranthine wind
      vanished inside the whirling
for a moment
we are one photon
in the eye of god.

The reference to the gnat inside the wind is from a Sufi story and poem by Rumi. The gnats complain to the great judge Solomon, champion of the little guys, that the winds are disrespectful: upon wind's arrival the gnats are simply blown away. Solomon, being just, calls for the East Wind to come and reply. When the wind arrives the gnats are entirely "vanished inside the whirling".

Human

We are composite
permeable form
a place
the world-spirit
travels through:

> minerals
>
> waters
>
> plants
>
> animals
>
> starfire
>
> wind

all these
gather fragments of humankind
carry bits of our genetic alphabet
downstream or disperse them
on dandelion filaments.

We greet these guests
> spirit embedded in world
tend them
as they flow through us
know that elements borrowed
from star-born
ancestors will be returned
for our children's
children.

To Honor the Four Directions

East

East births morning out
from tangible dark.
Hills blanketed in quiet
are naked, tender.
Pre-dawn's shadowless
glimmer is a reticent glow,
a sadhu at cave's mouth
singing to love
alone.

At night's edge
breezes stir
a wave of pearl-light
breaks against
the shore of day
      clouds are innocent as abalone
      birds sing like creation's first dawn
      human beings rise, pray, bow.

Earth's devotion to beauty washes

      through coastal wetlands
      where reeds shiver
      in crimson-tinged water

      through mangrove forests
      whose tigers wake
      and yawn

through open prairies as
sage grouse strut and fan.

Devotion
splashes against
rocky mountain shoulders

rolls through high
desert mesas

glances off sierran
glacial granite faces

turns coastal glass towers
to torches of magenta light.

Now a flood of gold envelops
serene and shadowed dark.

Yet, night remembers to
parse out
for each
tree, stone, stalk
house, human
to offer each one's daily
share of darkness.

Shadow
soft and diffuse
daylight's moon
is gift, cool relief;
it is mystery
the not-yet-known.
Light, in the end
brings paradox –

we bow
before shadow
differently
than we pray
to light

> Life without shade
> is lived on an anvil.

Night's cool follows us
as shadow
throughout the day
by the gift of
east's luminous face.

Many Indigenous peoples of the Americas offer ceremony and gratitude to the four di-
rections. I offer these poems as an inspiration for you to go to your favorite green place,
get on your knees and touch, smell, taste, see the minute details and recognize them as
fellow beings. Bow to the four corners of your life.

South

Appalachian July heat
takes hold
      slays us
      lays us down
      presses us into cool sand
dreaming
beside Mechum's river.

Bee balm grows
shoulder high
bumblebees stumble
among crimson petals
      intoxicated with nectar
      powdered by pollen.
Hummingbird moths
      ~ alluring imposters ~
court cone flowers
kiss black eyed Susans.
Wild begonias nod
in steamy southern sun.

August
heat ripens pawpaws,
possum paces through
heavy air
waits to taste their
sweet custard.
Wild turkey scratches
for beechnuts
reorganizes forest floor.
Rabbit chews scented catkins

while hazelnuts ripen
in their armored pod.

Mitochondria breathe
        create warmth by fire
        worship at sun god's altar.
Acolytes to this
combustive exultation
they will carry solar warmth
through winter's
inward reverie.

Southern sun's glory
        a furnace of love.
We carry this blast
in our star-born hearts.

West

Daylight's eve,
autumn forest beeches
slowly give way to splendor
day by day surrender
      cinnamon
      copper
      beaten gold
drench down each leaf
stem to tip.
Chlorophyll's emerald
summer display recedes
roots sprawl wide and shallow
dense thickets of
root-sprouted seedlings
lean close, clinging
while oak sapling's outsized leaves
leap red, shouting…look…look
and dogwood's
      arching branched fingers
      subtly articulate as our own
lift and bow.
Spine raised toward
blue winter's heaven,
limbs bend low
with generous touch
bring grace to
acorn stone lichen.

Autumn evening light
radiant
pours honey thick
upon late fall begonias

betrays their open green trust
as mercury drops
now one degree, now another.
Solomon's seal
in balanced wisdom
has decreed
a trove of gold-leaf
before frost's frigid furnace
blasts pitiless

carried on a clear white moon.

North

In winter dawn's pure
shadowless light
        mountain's north face
shapes emerge, recede.
Her slow pace stops
she bends
holds in her palm
the smooth
flat hip bone
        last winter's venison
weathered to a richly
embroidered surface.

She sees synaptic deltas
of her mind
reflected in bone's
fractalline calcium terrain.
Fingertips trace
its ivory in
ever repeating
diminishing
patterns.
She gazes soft, open.
Its infinite living form
refracts outward
visible in forest's
fine tapestry
        stone, mycelium, bark

Her branching
veins, arteries
are reiterated

in bare winter's
intricate, eloquent limbs
in reindeer moss
etched by crystals of frost
and velvet lichen
grown chocolate brown
on walnut trunk's
north side.

Sacred Earth ~ Sacred Self

*It is our task to imprint this temporary perishable earth into
ourselves so deeply, so painfully and passionately, that its
essence can rise again, invisibly, inside us. We are the bees of
the invisible. We wildly collect the honey of the visible, to store
it in the great golden hive of the invisible.*

RAINER MARIA RILKE

The devastation of ecosystems is but one symptom of the larger problem plaguing the earth. For hundreds of years Western culture has focused attention on the achievements of the individual person; we are taught to know who we are through individual attainment. Earlier cultures, though, recognized the individual as an essential organism within the functioning of the whole. During the 20th century and now two decades into the 21st, the dominant society's goal is to train the individual person to use their particular intelligence for the purpose of accruing ever more wealth and power, for their separate use and gratification.

Earth wisdom, however, affirms that in order to discover oneself a person needs to know who their ancestors are and where they have come from. Our *people* are carried in our genetic coding; the *land* shapes culture, therefore our own lives. Our people and our land give us a base-line orientation that guides us through all of life. Current brain science agrees: to thrive physically, emotionally, intellectually, and spiritually we need to be embraced by people: embedded in loving, attentive families and communities. We are designed to need, as well, regular immersion in the green earth and a living connection to a loving, guiding higher power.

> Let us rediscover our sacred self
> within the web
> of the sacred earth.
> Step outside;
> we find ourselves at one with
> ancient relatives of ours...
>
> > their waters are our waters
> > their winds, our breath

their plants, our food and medicines
their animals our teachers, friends, companions

They are still alive
well and functioning
not only in the world of nature
but within our own bodies

while silently
light
stardust
and minerals
flow through our veins.

Web

In forest light,
mind's kaleidoscope slows.
Movement germinates anew,
arising now from her feet
that step through leaf litter.

> *Solomon's Seal waves*
> *from a green ocean's*
> *distant reef.*
> *At her feet agrimony bows;*
> *hand to heart, she bends.*

Silken veils
invisibly spun across her path
reach out and cling to her,
as spiders come and greet .
Wrapped in webs she walks,
Spider Grandmother by her side.

> *Together they comb and spin Unity,*
> *weaving life's complexity*
> *from the singularity of One.*

A sole ray of light
pierces summer's canopy,
refracts off a silk thread
riding across her eyelashes.

It is an arrow of light
flying into the future
showing her the way.

Spider Grandmother is a central part of many American Indian creation myths. She helps to create life and remains with the people to guide and instruct them in respectful ways of being human.

Gestate

*The fire beetle mates only when the chaparral burns; the water beetle only in the
rain*

She is penetrated.
Emerald light passes
through skin and muscle
organ and bone.

> Brimming gold, light
> enters sycamore's leaf
> to emerge underside
> as prism-scattered
> shards of green.

Woman. Leaf. Both
 fertilized by light
gestated by breath.
Stem cells proliferate;
forms arise:

> *buds emerge.*
> *words are shaped.*

They are
foliate and literate ideas.

Carried by breezes,
new life is
a cradle rocked
on an ocean of green

Epigraph by Leah Green from The More Extravagant Feast

Belonging

Plant medicine flows in our blood.
Our brains mirror Pliocene acacias
we have lived beneath.
Language leaps through human synapses.
Intelligence moves
through phloem and xylem.

>   *I lean into the beech*
>   *resting against its*
>   *cool smooth skin.*
>   *Once I felt the sap*
>   *rising in subtle waves*
>   *pulsing against my forehead*
>   *pressed into its trunk.*

>   *I walk in forest's light.*
>   *Plant remedies in my veins*
>   *surge in recognition*
>   *of living relatives,*
>   *green beings I brush against.*
>   *A celebration ensues;*
>   *blood and sap are hoop-dancers*
>   *whirling in emerald light.*

Find starlight glinting in the mind
sunlight radiant in the heart.
Fireflies flicker in each cell
as electrons jump orbital loops.

Inhale lambent plant-light
   through the skin,
      its lustrous telluric glow.

Exhale radiant cosmic light
from the heart,
        incandescent lucent beams.

These two,
terrestrial and empyrean:

            light upon light,
            they choreograph
            resonant spheres
            within the body
             and shine
            into invisible worlds.

We are wedded light.
Walk a sacred circle,
nest in fields of belonging.

Flute

Wood thrush flutes
amid dogwood flowers.
Sings reality to me,
veils it in aeolian cadences.

She and I
inhabit this green cloister,
our lives spent among supple poplars.
They move by Appalachian winds
the way kelp forests billow in
clear shallows.

Repeating her spiral remembrance,
she is a Sufi clothed in simple brown.
I become dust at her delicate
crimson feet.

We take flight together;
sacred breath
inhabits my bones,
hollowed by the knife
of human limitations.
She, with bones made of air,
I with bones carved by grace,
our melody resonates in
the heart of the world.

"*The nightingale dips the truth into honey and makes this into poems*"
SHEIKH TAPDUK EMRE, 13TH CENTURY TEACHER OF
MYSTIC POET YUNS EMRE

Generations

bare February branches
bow to cold winds
chimes chant prayers

summer's hydrangea stalks
rattle sun-drenched thoughts
that skitter past frozen ferns

cardinals call from
dogwood's silver branches
etched into winter's brocade

poplar and spicebush
hickory and beech
employ mycelial spinners who

thread by thread
weave arboreal
connective tissue

make a living membrane
between pine and oak
red maple and magnolia

bring nutrition
give warning
nurse illness

      interspecies collaboration,
      or can we finally see
      it is love.

My feet walk and sing,
I bow to
Gaian ancestors

who arise through
my soles
enter into human veins

which are not unlike
those of
sugar maple leaves

alluvial spirits reweave
my connective tissue
make a living plasma

mend places
torn by the past
and weave as well
toward the future

> interspecies collaboration,
> or can I finally say
> *this is love.*

Footfall

I.
The gong calls
> come to vastness
> to silence
pull back the veil
enter gracious emptiness.

She paces toward the hall
presses blessings down
one footstep at a time.

> In hopes that prayer
> will leave fossil remains.
> Each footfall
> one diatom of peace.

> In hopes to leave
> a subtle layer
> of sedimented grace
> laid down into soft loam
> that a millennia hence
> will continue
> to nourish generations.

> Each step is one wish
> among numberless
> prayer-diatoms.
> Peace piles up
> beneath sycamore roots
> and quartz outcroppings,
> makes a fine
> nutrient-laden lining

below green and gold pebbles
in White Branch Creek's
stream bed.

II.
In the years
of stepping through
time beyond time
stone by stone
her skin has now
grown thin enough:

emerald blessings come
flashing up
from roots and lichen.
Bursts of love,
they are fireflies blinking
through a star-drenched sky.

Each footfall is a benediction and
brings holy replies
given by ancestors and close kin
       lime stone
       soil bacteria
       black walnut
          with her pungent scent
       woodpecker
          the insistent knock
       a thousand crickets
          who sing in dawn's blush.

Till a river of morning stars
dip down from the Milky Way
to rush and eddy
through her blood.

The gong is singing
in her veins.

*Diatoms are single-celled algae that live in houses made of glass: their cell walls are
composed of transparent, opaline silica, ornamented in intricate, striking patterns.
Microscopic, they produce 50% of the air we breathe, feed the oceans, lakes and rivers,
and tell us of the health of the waters. There are vast deposits of diatomaceous earth all
around the globe.*

Doorway

We are tori.
Oscillating,
we are the wedding
of heaven and earth
cosmic and corporeal.

> *Embedded in earth*
> root-sprouting toes are kin
> to mycellial fruit.

> Arms reach to
> *touch sun's fire,*
> cherry limbs stretch
> to gather light.

> *Seeded by stars*
> diamond heart's radiance
> is firmament's child.

> *Nebula-flung minerals*
> flow through our veins,
> electrolytes illumine
> synaptic conversation.

The body is a fractal.
It maps the
sacred geometry
where mystery occurs.

We are a doorway
between the worlds.

The Torus shows us how energy moves in its most balanced dynamic flow process.
Toroidal energy fields exist around everything: people, trees, the earth, the sun...every-
thing. Pioneering researcher Arthur Young says "The self in a toroidal Universe can be
both separate and connected with everything else." Science is catching up with ancient
wisdom. Fractals are infinitely unfolding symmetry, and they are present everywhere.

This Breath Ocean

To ride the winds
~ god's breath ~
is to abide by laws
we do not understand

     laws written by soil
     ~ mineral-laden from Saharan winds
     blown across the Atlantic ~
     to sustain lush tropic fruit

     laws pulled from mile-deep
     salt fissures off Antarctic ice
     washed through South Pacific seas
     making phytoplankton bloom
     and krill feast

     laws governing
     cascading synesthesia
     a kaleidoscope as raucous
     fertile, densely nuanced
     as rainforests in Amazonia

     laws printed in
     remnants of stars
     and genetic coding.

This cannot be breathed
as the first three kinds
of remembrance:
Not like the vast round
"there is no reality but god."

Not the insistent hammer
"only god, only god."
Not the lover's
whispered duet
"god is lover and beloved."
These are woven of
I and Thou
make a safe haven
for the *breather*.

This breath-ocean is for
the breathed, alone

      manta ray, porpoise
      acacia, live oak
      have been *the breathed*
      through millennia

      a sandpiper runs on matchstick legs
      a pelican plummets into waves
      the calm sea swells and falls
      it is breathed
            now in
            now out.

Yet we must sigh
"*let go, let go*"
a silent petition to
commingle with
the breathed.

Till finally
we come to know
the only place for "I,"

in the great respiration,
is to be effaced into

"I Am."

This is not the "I Am" that we read in the Bible; not an idea separated from the life that embodied beings inhabit. This is the true speech of the living world. Truth is written by the sacred sounds the mycorrhizal networks repeat. It is carried in phloem and xylem, to exude as leaf-born truth: light, sugar, oxygen. This is the actual lived-reality of the I Am into which we dissolve.

Prana

Mother to earth's water cycle
breath is an airborne ocean
moving through
tissue, muscle, blood.

The woman is made new
at each in-breathing;
her scent, note, hue are
given away
at each out-breathing.

She becomes a river bed:
her stones, minerals, bones
sculpt the shape of water.

She breathes the earth,
calls it inside her body:

> the coyote by night
> at stream's confluence
> gnawing bones,
> catching crayfish

> grandchildren by day
> splashing, squabbling;
> stream ripples glisten
> in sunlight

> owl calls to her mate,
> the woman motionless
> is sheltered by pines.

Her mind, prayer, heart
flow out on the breath.

Earth and woman are
twined as lovers;
each one's embrace
subtly shapes and
molds the other,
their rhythms rising
and falling in tandem.

An Aeolian harp
~ her strings tuned by unseen hands ~
it is her melody that
pleases the wind.

Essence

Meaning radiates,
inherent in particle,
wave, chemical collaboration.
This gift is grace that
holds me unceasingly in its thrall.
Each day my heart asks
what is the meaning of

>galaxies of wildflowers
>shining in emerald orbit;
>landscapes printed into lavender
>turkey-tail mushrooms;
>pebbles radiant in evening light;
>wine berry's barb,
>wood thrush's flute?
>what does black fly show me
>washing her front legs as carefully
>as I brush my hair?

I listen, while White Branch Creek explains,
uttering psalms through Paleozoic ferns,
then turn to the nations of birds;
the chorus of goldfinches
in treetop aviaries, who
repeat their infinite canon.

I ask the breezes who rustle
ever-responsive leaves
>slender wild cherry
>beech's pleated skirts
>red bud's green heart
"What news? Of what seagoing affairs

do you tell
with your plankton-born air?"

Sight, sound, touch, smell
usher the living earth
directly inside my skin.
They are living transformations.
       Chrysalides within my soul
       they return to life's primordial ooze,
       evolve gossamer wings,
and I arise into sacred meaning.

Animalia II

I've spent the day in our forest gardens pulling poison ivy, clipping back wild roses, pulling mile-a-minute at the root. Now I need open fields and slanted evening rays.

I walk the farm road. The fields are wide, with the damp smell of a recent mow. The light changes nearly imperceptibly, my feet move slow and steady. I gaze, breathing the sweeping openness.

This is when I see a diffuse gray-brown shadow on the distant hillside field. The field is dotted with cows and new calves, but this is nothing domesticated. Its stealth belies something feral; its agency and skill bent toward its own wild uses. Slowly my brain adjusts and I see the fox. But this is the great-granddaddy of all foxes: bigger, shaggier, long fleecy tail.

I am quiet, taking him in with all my senses; he defies sight alone. Now he feels me feeling him: stops mid-step, ears alert, gazing across the field at me. We stand suspended, breathing each other's breath for minutes outside of time. I feel him search me, palpating for my intention. Satisfied at last, he turns back to his business at hand. I watch as he bounds off appearing and disappearing amid the tall grass and hillocks. I am honored to have been seen by him.

Now it has become twilight; cool exudes from the earth. At the crossing of a small stream I notice several barn swallows hunting the evening air. One of them catches my eye, the one with a pure white wing feather. He is arcing, looping, diving toward the insects hovering above the slow waters. He shoots out across the hillside with speed and power, then soars up in high rounds, ready to dive again. I begin to laugh; his joy in flight and the hunt is contagious. He notices my attention, draws his acrobatic loops closer and places me in his sights. He comes wheeling toward me, veers to the left and wraps an arc of swift air around me, then whizzes away. Utterly transfixed, I am laughing out loud. Time elongates as he plays with me, targets me, dodges and delights me. My laughter urges him on to finer feats.

It seems a long time later I catch a slight movement from the corner of my eye. A simple brown rabbit is hopping on the road toward me. I am surprised she hasn't noticed me, hasn't frozen in fear. She continues to hop close to me; I finally speak to her and she pauses. I bend and hold out my hand to her, the way years ago I called my house rabbits to come. She now hops directly to me, stopping only a few feet away. We stand together in the evening air as clouds turn rose and lavender against the powder-blue sky. I talk quietly with her about her beauty and courage to come so close. Again, I open my arms to her. She hesitates, deciding, then turns sideways and with a final glance proceeds along her evening mission.

I gaze upward to find the swallows again. Suddenly one separates from the others and comes diving my way. We're at the game again, until finally dark begins to close the day. He returns to the hunt; I turn toward home ~ humble, grateful, speechless.

Time. Space.

Not immutable,
time expands, carried on
      daylight's progression
      of shadows,
      waves of birdsong and
      springtime balm.

Time contracts;
it is moonlit owls,
autumn leaf musk,
February snow.
.

Not empty,
space is embodied by living systems
      mychorrizal networks
      amazon's flying rivers
      salmon who carry
            sea nutrients upstream
            to fertilize coastal forests.

Space is ripe with song-lines;
melodies of pre-eternal treaties
between land and peoples.

        ****

Blood traveling water ways
through my veins
knows these truths.
Knowledge percolates through
my body, the way trees share
nutrition through stones, and

send pheromone warnings
 on the breeze.

Forest wisdom, held by
other-than-human-persons,
cascades as chemical communications
through my limbs,
circulates as blood and breath.

       ★★★★

Concepts of mind
bow low before
sight, sound, scent, touch,
before movement and silence.
I fold concepts inward
toward the heart;
let them open outward
into land, wind, fertile deltas.

Concepts pray.
They long to be, finally,
skin to skin with life.

April Eve

Densely patterned forest light,
evening's ample brocade,
is child born of confluences ~
galactic forces whose ancient play
became this primordial fold
of Appalachian ore,
as mountain spirit rolled
in his textured igneous bed.

This cleft,
wide enough for
a single arrow of light
loosed from the solar bow,
illumines a newly viridian
spring glade, a humble place
of human proportion,
at Blue Mountain's feet

And I was still a girl
when I first stepped
into its emerald ray.
There I stood transfixed,
light's silken fabric
undulating through
poplar and cherry leaves.
Decades later I remain so.
Transformed.
New as the
springtime evening light.

A History of Fire

Birth

A child drifts like mist;
dayscapes within
home, prairie
her father's garden.
Dreamscapes hold
open thresholds
a bee hive
the night sky.

This is liquid wandering,
fluid as mandarin fish
gliding through Pacific coral.
Her parents say
"In her own little fog."

Until the time of fire.

Initiation

Seared, scorched, scoured
charred to ash,
her house of self
is burned to the ground.

She is incense for the gods:
grassland soil, elm roots
fields of wheat
bees in clover:
sweet, pungent
tart, earthen.

Elements harvested
through her twenty years
now lit by holy fire
burn hot, concentrated
a single point of scarlet
till what remains is
fragrant white ash.

Silence

Breath echoes
through inner space.
A vast empty cavern,
she must know.
Amid firestorm's ruin
she will learn
to keep the flame.

Fire-Keeper

Certain seeds open
only in conflagration
yet must be saved
from coal and ash.

Bare hands
retrieve seeds.
Rinse, soak
set to simmer
at the back
with onions and garlic
green herbs
her ground bones.

She crafts
the well-sealed vessel
learns to watch and tend.

Fire Wall

Concrete and steel beams:
daily prayer and practice.
She builds the wall
partitioning her heart.

On the hot side
unabated flames
day and night
decade by decade.
The combustion
of her intention
lineage, breath
the relentless
slow inferno burns.

She has vowed
to never be ambushed
by smallness again
to be as large
as she must
to pay the price, whatever.

On the warm side
she tends her kitchen fire
she learns
to taste and season
to stir little and
simmer long.

She learns by beauty
inspiration
impetus, capacity.
She learns
by garden days
children's quarrels
bedtime prayers.

She makes a life of
beneficence and love
calls sons home from
forest tromping.
With baths, table napkins
and graces sung
she domesticates their
feral days
calls them into
       storied
       complex
       complicit
the culture of man.

She is a salamander
in the fire
ever burning
ever maintaining.

Lumen

Fire's inferno blazes scarlet
its volcanic destruction
       consumes dross
       forges light.

Birthed by the sun
she
      makes star-fire
      into sweet sustenance.

Sacred Dreams

Humans grow ever more human, as they become an expression of the world. They find themselves, not by seeking themselves, but by uniting themselves to the world in love.

RUDOLF STEINER

Enter Healing Waters

Dreams arrive, washed up onto the shores of the conscious mind. They bring the star flowers of sea grass, and kelp's rich minerals. Like plankton, they are carried on life's saline currents bringing crucial nourishment.

By night I wonder, am I a whale.... a river dolphin? Or perhaps another cetacean ~ mammals that evolved on land, but longed for life's original home in warm ocean currents. I sleep as they do, in unihemispheric slow wave sleep: half the brain asleep rocked by the pull of the moon while the other half remains wakeful, watching. A mind in each deep current, one part rests regenerated in liminal organic images: these compose the archetypal riverbeds ~the bloodstream ~ for the body of Gaia. The other mind listens for language, to craft a spoken container subtly alive, malleable enough to call these wild image-beings into partnership, collaboration.

Come, immerse yourself with me in these mystic waters. Here you will find stardust, beneficial insects, adobe ruins, thermal water, Mongolian steppes. Perhaps these images will seed your night-ocean and you will find lustrous pearls layering up inside your being. Together we will dream the visions of Gaia herself; midwife these dreams into realities. Let this be a water-birth, rocked in psyche's deep oceanic cradle.

Adobe in Three Parts

One:
Turn around
see the house of
night breezes,
star-strewn sky.
Pristine
white on white
it is a waltz
of straight and curve
intimacy formed
in place,
life tucked into a bower.

Two:
Adobe
house of spirits
the one we began
when we were
young and round
like Eden's first two leaves
that tender house of earth.
Now inner walls dissolve
ashes to ashes.
It is ruin
an earthen palace
turning again to clay.
Dust motes drift gold,
blanket open emptiness.

Three:
Ground squirrels and
ants burrow in.
Children dwell here;
they do not know
to re-mud walls at the
moon-when-leaves-break-forth.
The kiva is unbroken but
they do not know to pray.
Sacred Animal Spirits come,
messengers of primal wisdom.
They bring the sacred ceremonies.
The sacred circle thrives.

It is Night

It is night. They come, thick
muscular. Their undulations
~ sinuous alert power ~
are waves made flesh.
Male and female, the snakes
are horizontal melodies
in a terrestrial fugue.

The woman's ancient brain
hears their music:
        knowledge evolves by epochs
        gestated in seawater
        birthed into bacteria
        coiled up as mollusks
        till one moment in time
        perception migrates
        to dry land and
        wisdom lives buried, burrowed
        layered in soil carbon
        sequestered by nematodes and fungi,
        by wild grace.

Recognizing ancestral kin,
she sees intelligence glide toward her.
A primal synaptic leap and
she steps toward them
        to shelter from harm
        from two-legged fear of
        a garden
          an apple
            eternal eviction.

To protect fluid-knowing
~ serpentine gestalt ~
from the metal blade of a shovel.

She stands at the
crack in the world
carries oneness in her body
reaches out.

She holds snake's
weight and length
in her hand.
Woman and viper are
curious intelligence.

Navigating by scent
he brushes past her hair
catches molecules, pheromones,
orients toward her.
She knows now.
Hurry.

For transport and refuge
she needs
a container to hold them
   well-sealed for inward journeying,
a vehicle to carry them
   well-oiled for whatever terrain.

All is prepared.
Only now does she see
the marks of the pit viper.
Her arm, hot, swells.
Only now does she see
their bodied exchange

as he moves forward
with human legs
while she, full of
snake medicine, begins.

Bee

The skirt is bell-like.
Round, it is a tulip.
Now the heat: bee stings.
A hive of bees swarm
under petals made of silk.

She lies down
her legs
pollen-rich stamen
her pelvis a pod
ripened by bee-heat.

A thousand
red hot points,
skin splits a
thousand times.
Black living seeds
burst out.

Biography in Dreams

Stardust
Stars migrate through black sky.
Constellating, they are
alphabet to a primal tongue
spoken by coral
mycelium, embryos.

These words are spoken
into the neural core of her being.

Mineral
Hillside forest.
Spider webs are quilted sunlight.
Her veins open into this dawn.
Tourmaline crystals
tumble at her feet.

She is mineral.

Plant Woman
Her ancestral home
succumbs to fecund
silted flood waters.
A chair rocks slowly.
Lavender grows
in the palm of her hand.

Waters slowly rise.

Plant Milk
The child lies heavy
ripe in her womb.

Waiting, she kneels
plants lettuce, peas, basil.
Soon holding him
her new mother's milk
flows green.

The child smiles, asleep.

Sea Mammal
Woman, she undulates in
primordial waters.
Lambent pearls
cascade across her body.
Threads of pearl-light
become a map;
her body traces the
shape of matter.

Worlds seen and unseen.

Beneficial Insect
A child, she climbs stairs
spiraling ever up
ascends hand over hand
searches high above
~a vaulted skylight~
perceives the honey bee
   wants the golden drop
      reaches into mid-air
echoing chasm below.

Outstretched, she leans.

Land Animal
Her hair becomes silk banners,
flags flying in mist-laden wind.

She dances on tiger's back.
Jungle fronds sway,
green waves parting

as the she-tiger passes.

Earth
Cretaceous sea beds
become black earth.
The prairie is her body.
In repose, she notices song birds
prairie dogs, quail
who nest in her tall grass.

Moving across the horizon
a slow fire approaches.

She smiles.

Carbon Redemption

Petroleum runs
through childhood streets.
On the chain gang
she mops black tar.
Life a billion years old,
she scrubs it with
rags and tears.
She kneels scouring,
praying.
What is the
mystery of forgiveness?

A new gang boss,
hat pulled low
leads her away.
His hands
tender
guide her into
quiet thermal waters.
He speaks as mother
to weeping child
in tones low and soft.
They play like children
like long time lovers.
God pours through
her laughter.

I was born in a small Kansas town, in the midst of wheat country. Family farms and farm towns died quickly in the wake of chemical fertilizers, pesticides, herbicides and mass debt incurred by the "new farming." The economy of my town was kept stable by an oil refinery: this economic solution was and remains part and parcel of the funda-mental destructive paradigm.

Dream Ache

The woman gathers
pieces of colored glass.
Though translucent shards,
she sees them
with a gardener's eye.
Refracted light,
she collects each
shade by shade
as though plucking blooms
for an autumn tea.

Each piece
becomes a note of birdsong
as it glances into her bowl.
Perhaps it is
a singing bowl filled with
petals of light.
So you understand
her surprise
when she sees the blood.

She had only wished
to taste the luscious colors
to swallow and feel them
course through her veins.
Only wished the luminescence
would shine through her pores.
Or hoped to awaken as a bee
to drink in sunlight and
exude honey.

Mongol

She is a child.
On high steppes
she follows her flock.
Pure, she is the land,
as are her sheep
      one seamless whole
      woven by grace.

The people fear her.
She speaks, laughs
shares food
plays with brothers.
Still the fear
the awe.

It is because of her eyes,
her pleasure with solitude.
It is because she sings
alone
      with boundless swell of grasses
      with sheep
      whirring insects
      sighing wind
      refracted sunlight
      with starry spheres
      revolving in magisterial rounds
      whirling through her child's body.
Alone, she sings.

The people do not know this song.
They fear.

You sing the
names of Spirit, child
sing the original tongue.
It is the first language
spoken long before humans,
known by nebula
DNA, diatoms.
It is a syntax of
sea water and coral.

You speak the lyrics of
our ancestors
as they left
arboreal homes
learned to tread
firm earth.

You sing a hymn that is
painted on cave walls
printed into clay pots
woven into tapestries
by gnarled, knowing hands.
You sing the names of God.

Next day at dawn
she dresses
sips bitter tea
rocks her baby brother
eats the bowl of grain.
She goes alone
with all created beings
into her grassland refuge.
She sings.

Snake

She holds a surprise, a gift.
With eager love
she shelters it from view
under her loose shirt.
Her beloved comes close.
Heart pounding
she brings a posy out
into the light.
It is a bridal bouquet.
Woven together at the tail
she holds a garland of
rainbow snakes.
Lovers and serpents
dance slow motion
in the sun.

Invitation

Something calls
from the sphere of night:
enigmatic as the song dog's melodies
  drifting down from the high orchard
  on night's breeze,
visceral as the egg
  who calls to one sperm among all others,
  opening a secret door to the unknown.

A secret door lies between
landscapes of light and viscous dark.
Persephone's daughter,
queen of the dead, goddess of fertility
steps through into Eleusinian mystery:
  a chrysalis
  not dead
  not yet alive.
Held, spun in silk wrappings
she waits.

A small jewel ~ a truth ~
refracts outward
to shape the world of form.

A fractal builds outward
from lucid beginnings,
becomes ever more complex;
its pure core
remains true in each
geometrically repeating form.

Mycorrhiza live this truth
as does the
redwing blackbird
who broadcasts her
singular signature
on an insistent trill.

Dream Speech

A young boy listens
hears bass, baritone voices
of a broad flat river,
soprano notes made by
eddies and stony bottomed curves.
He whispers,
repeating these river-words;
one foot in each world
~ fluid and earthen ~
he translates.

The woman holds reins
loosely in her hand.
The horse knows the way.
It is a promenade:
she, the horse, her sister.
She speaks aloud
the boy's whispered words.
Her sister
relaxed in the saddle
is content;
the horse sways
beneath her thighs.
A silk blindfold
tied round her eyes,
its tasseled corners
mingle with her
unbound hair
ruffled by
a sometimes breeze.

Her breath is quiet
slowly paced
in union with the horse;
low afternoon light
penetrates the silk and
her own silken eyelids.
She sees the shadows play
  across her closed eyes
  shades of coral, gold, rose
  change with high
  drifting clouds:
  the light inside the dark.
She hears the river's voice
  the boy's translated whispers
  her twin's words.
  Wind in treetops
  echoes river speech.

People glance as the
archetypes slowly pass by.

Humans can bear
so little truth.
We pause
take one sip of elixir,
then turn back toward our
commonplace work.

Ever abiding

  river
  boy
  horse
  sisters

Steadily, they know the way.

Earth Unfolding

I.

This dream unfolds in epochs; I am both witnessing outside of the dream and actively involved in each scene. Enigmatic melodies drift through; I hear

> sea
> song-thrush
> worker bees sweating wax
> into six-sided chambers
> silk being spun from
> larval saliva
> pine-scented wind
> the nervous system's
> synaptic compositions

Throughout eons of time, I both see and am in the midst of vast herds of grazing animals. As Witness, I see the migrating herds are a mammalian ocean: waves of warm blood rise and fall in synchronous patterns, gracing grasslands, and fertilizing beauty, season by season. *Inside* the herd, I am in the jostling lovely responsive body contact. We move with one mind, the way flocks of birds play in autumn winds. This movement is archetypal; each animal-nation moving according to it own rhythm of stars and seasons. The planet is awash in herds birthing, grazing, migrating, dying, cycling through infinite meaning and time. They are waves in one continuous ocean of flesh, populating new savannas. Schools of vibrant fish swell, and forage in mineral-rich seawater.

II.

Painted dogs, not-yet-wolves, come barking. Their calico ears furl open, upright like new spring leaves, swiveling for sound. Heads low, paws forward, their tails wag an invitation. I run toward them and realize I also am four-legged!

I leap forward to play,
to breed, care, hunt
unified for millennia
with canids
traversing continents,
the land-bridge.

Millennia later, I see that sticks have been arranged on the steppes
and prairies. They have been prepared for the herds to move through.
The Witness understands this is the work of the first proto-humans;
it is intentional and information-gathering. They are assessing the
health and life-force of the herds.

Now these bipeds come to us, we dogs, and invite us to become their
allies. We understand this as good: our strength, speed and physical
prowess harnessed to the brilliance of a mind we have never before
encountered.

Much later ~ a hundred thousand years? ~ the Witness sees the two-
leggeds, now become human, begin to search for other animals to
invite into affiliations. Other-than-human people are pleased and
make offerings to them:

     Wolf, who made the world
     perfects their hunt.
     Horse, gift of the stars
     is their relative.
     White Buffalo Calf Woman
     brings food, clothing
     shelter, brings the gift
     of the sacred pipe

Epochs arise, ensue, transform. Animal and human, together we live
the original instructions. These collaborations are the embodiment
of truth and beauty.

III.

Until the membrane of unity is ripped. Twentieth century humans ~ no longer innocent ~ cleave apart pristine species-alliances, venerate competition and domination reigns. Decades of fossil fuels and climate change rush life toward the brink. Amid extraction and plunder, a cancer spreads. It contaminates water, poisons soils, fouls the wind.

> No longer does spirit-breath
> speak freely.
> No wind horse carries souls.
> Bird languages disappear
> beneath oil-drenched opulence.

We are no longer in the natural world. We are in some grandiose indoor space. Gilded doors, sealed against the green blessings of the natural world, control the climate and human minds as well. We are no longer natural beings, but are completely removed from our embryonic dependence upon the living world. Lavish food spills off platters into people's silk-suited laps. Bored, indolent eyelids drooping, humanity's thick lazy stupidity fills the air.

I notice a young man's eyes flicker alive for a moment. He says haltingly "I remember a time when it was not like this....I remember... something else...." The young man he is talking with responds "I, as well... have heard a story about another time..." An older man is eating and drinking lavishly. He laughs uproariously, drooling his food. "Who wants a different time?" The young men struggle to hold this fleeting awareness amidst the dense atmosphere.

I awaken with the sick feeling of corporate greed in the pit of my stomach. I roll over and go back to sleep:

IV.
Stand with me on this bridge between times
        between *what has been* and
        what wants to be born.
V.

Now I am with a group of people somewhere in Asia. It is the time of ceremony. The Empress is to have her feet washed; the gilt basin is ready. I have been chosen to enact this ceremony with her, and am informed of the immense importance of this honor. She waits regally.

I am given a large water vessel but at my approach, she playfully pulls her feet up under her robes. Now we are twinkling and quietly laughing together. Amidst coaxing and playfulness, she slowly lowers her feet to be washed in the warm clear waters.

A smaller bowl is now given. It is a rich composite: frankincense, precious minerals, black deep-prairie soil. I am to pour it into the pristine water. As I wash her feet, I watch the elixir spiral around the basin:
        See
           clouds
           wave patterns
           fractal's swirl
           orbiting interplanetary dust
        See
           evolution emerging
           in generative waters

The foot-washing cleanses, blesses, and nourishes everyone. We are given wafers now, to immerse in the germinating elixir, to eat and thereby absorb grace.

        this is Her body,
        this is Her blood

this is a new
Holy Communion

Now, the washing finished, I turn to bring her shoes. Upon return I
see

her feet bare
unbound
even by silken shoes.
She steps down and,
arms outstretched,
runs lightly away from
glistening marble
ornately carved wood

away
from the prison
of separation.
Hair unclasped
flowing free behind her
lustrous in forest's green light
she runs *home*
as a thrush sings in
the scented woods.

*Earth Unfolding, a dream, searches for scent, melody, living images: to point us
toward a new way of seeing humanity's long past, and fresh hope for a return to the
feminine principle of relationship with all beings*

Litany is Ceremony

*A group can practice this Gaian Litany together.
It is inspired by my childhood's European Litanies, Sufi
practices of calling the Names of God, as well as the
Haudenosaunee "Words Spoken Before All Others,"
also called the Iroquois Thanksgiving.*

It is the twenty first century. We have wrenched the Sacred from her tellurian home; exiled her beyond the blue earth, the benevolent trees, and our bronze flesh. Drowning in wealth, we ache and grieve, alone in night's dark hour, asking "why?" Why this hollow echo inside, why the flat emptiness of life, why this lonely despair?

Yet all the while, there is another way, just outside the door. The perfumed spring-time forest beckons, her elegant flowers are calling us away from the cyber-chains that bind us. A white-tail deer glimmers between tree trunks, stopping to turn liquid eyes toward us. Birds wait to sing for us, each note a doorway to truth. Step into earth's sanctuary and begin to know the nature of each being, the qualities of each plant medicine. Learn the names and ways of these other than human persons ~ this litany of wild saints. Bring joy and gratitude. Call the names of these beings; know they are listening, they understand. The language of the heart needs no translation. May this litany be

> *Invocation; to call forth*
> *other-than-human presences.*
>
> *Invitation; to join in the great*
> *conversation of beings.*
>
> *Participation in a living*
> *geography*
> *botany*
> *zoology*
> *cosmology*
> *a vocabulary of Oneness.*

This is litany in its most untamed and fecund form. Call the names of

> *land formations*
> *water mothers*
> *plant beings*
> *animal cousins*
> *fire spirits.*

A ripple of gratitude echoes toward the past, refracts into the future. The long round of time glistens with a thread of human remembrance.

> *Litany is creative word*
> *Word is animate being*
> *Being is the breath that sings*
> *among us.*

Let us sing their names as we walk.

The Litany

Geography: Land Forms

Red rock canyon
Appalachia's igneous core
Sand susurration
Speaking stones
Breathing earth
Sand, silt
Tourmaline, jasper

Together, we are whole

Rock face
Sacred stone
Native soil
Wind-sculpted bluffs
Sandstone tower
Mineral strata
Holy ground

Together, we are whole

Encircling stones
Mountain bowl
Land sculpts mind
Folding, forested hills
Riverbank and raccoon
Seashore and pelicans
Equatorial deltas

Together, we are whole

Geography: Water Mothers

Rain as grace
Creek water eddies
Ice diamonds fall
Winter's white silence
Volcanic hot spring
Mist-laden pond
Water cress blooms
Pure groundwater

Together, we are whole

Epic floods
Tears rain inside her body
Rip-tide swirl
Water protectors sing
Hurricane rains
Water is life
Salish Seas Salmon Nation

Together, we are whole

Northern blue ice mountains
Tidal salt marshes
Spirit seeps
Currents of a natural mind
Hydrating neural highways
Pummeled by surf
Pause in tidal pools

Together, we are whole

Botany: Plant Beings

Rain-calling trees
Poplar's netted roots
Translucent Indian Pipe
Morel mushrooms
Lavender raspberry canes
Beech nut, curly dock
Garlic mustard, fiddlehead fern

Together, we are whole

Copper beech branches
Silver glade fern
Light-eating chloroplasts
Native spicebush
Mycellial networks
Jack-in-the-Pulpit
Moist glade

Together, we are whole

Wineberry
Paw-paw
Hazelnut
Trillium
Foliated holy trinity
Arboreal spirit
Veins as phloem

Together, we are whole

Zoology; Animal Cousins

Mulberry worms spinning
Sea birds crying
Predators keep the balance
Herds migrating
Ruby-throated hummingbird
Worm-knowing
Sparrow singing

Together, we are whole

Bouquet of living snakes
Diamond antlered stag
Herds, packs
Flocks, schools
Damselfly suspended above stream
Peacock preens
Bear cub paw prints

Together, we are whole

Coyote's choral singing
Red fox's night barking
Bobcat shrieks
Redwing blackbird feeds
Quail hen's feint
Winged honey-guides call
Owl's gabbling

Together, we are whole

Primate ancestors
Microbes
Segmented worms

Cricket cadence
Dawn geese
Wood thrush's crimson feet
Chambered nautilus
Drops of blood

Together, we are whole

Fire Spirits

Star dust
Mitochondrial fire
Quartz crystal
Tongues of flame
Sun mysteries
Love's light alone
Sun-being rays out

Together, we are whole

Father of all incandescence
Light gifted by fire
Destruction eclipsed by grace
Communion of light upon light
Steamy southern sun
Mitochondria worship
Sun-gods altar
Combustive exaltation

Together, we are whole

Furnace of joy
Seared, scorched, scoured
Charred to ash
Burn to the ground

Incense for the gods
Lit by the holy fire
Fire-storm's ruin

Together, we are whole

Fire-keeper
Combustion of intention
Slow inferno burns
Flames blaze scarlet
Birthed by the sun

Together, we are whole

Breath of God

Imprint of wind
Conjoined Spirit
Oxygen cycles through time
Breath is tender sharing
Vapor, breeze,
Gust, zephyr
Child of god

Together, we are whole

Howling wind
Living air
Vanished inside the whirling
Amaranthine wind
Moonlit breeze
Wind-rustled grass
Spirit languages

Together, we are whole

Glimmering in thin air
Breath is a layered elixir
The wind of our passing

Together, we are whole

"Something sacred is coming this way.

"That is how my ancestors would have said it. In the midst of all this turmoil and confusion, when we cannot clearly see the path before us, when we feel trapped in a situation we cannot control, then I believe the wise elders of my holy heritage would climb to the high place of the heart, draw the circle of reason and faith around them, and stand to sing their prayers into the open sky of the history to come.

They would not shrink into a corner afraid, but rise up to catch the first light of what was coming into being all around them."

THE RT. REV. STEVEN CHARLESTON, CHOCTAW NATION